ADVANCED

MANIFESTING

The Magic of Manifesting
Your Dreams from Reel Life

By Primrose Roberts

ADVANCED MANIFESTING

The Magic of Manifesting
Your Dreams from Reel Life

© 2022 by Primrose Roberts

https://primroseroberts.com/

https://advancedmanifestingacademy.com/

Disclaimer

DEDICATION

To Calinda, Kyle, and Charlotte

TABLE OF CONTENTS

"Who looks outside, dreams.
Who looks inside, awakens."

~ Carl Jung

Awaken and Fulfill Your Dreams Now

Born into a world of obstacles

Where there is no gain without pain

For life is a battle where champions take the medals.

A life where every day dawns into challenges

As everyone is called to be an avenger.

Toiling in the rain and hoping for the sun

For only when the sun shines is hay made

Yet the rain and stormy weather remain the order of the day

Success becomes a dream suffocating in the vacuum of difficulties

Which ends up making you stay in slumber.

Naivety is not an excuse

For opportunities are like open doors

Where failure to locate them entails exclusion from the banquet

As only the go-getters will wine and dine

While daydreamers toil in drought and famine.

Yes, life is a jungle yet there is a king and a pride

Take the strike and catch your prey

For no dream comes from space

But from within where realities emanate

Awaken, face your fears and fulfill your dreams now.

CHAPTER 1

RECREATE YOUR REALITY

(M is for "Midnight in Paris")

What if you were magically granted one wish – and no, you can't wish for more wishes – what will it be? How will it materially change your life? What kind of person do you expect to become?

The truth about wishes is that most people spend their lives searching for the secret to manifesting their dreams but fail to notice the answer is hidden in plain sight—at the movies.

You merely need to look beyond the screen to discover that great movies present myriad possibilities of how to achieve your goals and fulfill your dreams. It's no wonder Shakespeare was inspired to declare: "*All the world's a stage, and all the men and women merely players…*"

After all, if everyone is subject to an underlying master narrative, what role are you playing? Is it true to type? Can you flip the script?

If you pay close attention, you'll discover that a movie hero follows a specific formula to achieve his goals in reel life. This allows him to move from rags to riches, pain to pleasure, and defeat to victory.

Once you gain a better understanding of the "reel world," it will help you better navigate the real world.

Which begs the question: Why do we find movies so appealing? It may be because their stories speak about universal themes that resonate with us.

They orient us to what is valuable and essential in life: family, faith, freedom, love, honor, courage, goodness, and justice.

They teach us the right way to act. They give us glimpses into the flaws and potentialities of human nature. They evoke emotions that inspire us to change so we too can live the good life.

Once you take a closer look at the movies, you'll notice there's more to reel life than meets the eye. In fact, it almost mirrors real life in that the plot is based upon the law of cause and effect, which means the hero first desires something and then must take action to obtain it.

The ensuing story reveals the goal the hero is motivated to pursue, the actions she takes to achieve it, the price she's willing to pay for it, and how the experience transforms her.

What drives the story forward is the unfolding narrative of the hero's pursuit of her goal. We become drawn to the outcome as a moth to a flame. We align with the hero and become willing participants in the drama onscreen as we recognize different aspects of ourselves.

Whatever obstacles she encounters and fights to overcome elicit similar emotions in us. When she suffers, we suffer; when she loves, we love; when she wins, we win.

Similarly, we may have our own goals and aspirations that we wish to fulfill in real life. As we make known our desires to the Universe, we find ourselves unwittingly embroiled in the ensuing drama in relation to it against our will.

As each scenario unfolds with its own plotline and plot twists, we feel compelled to take specific actions—overcome certain obstacles—play shifting roles to achieve our goal. Win or lose, we are transformed by the experience.

"Nostalgia is denial – denial of the painful present … the name for this denial is golden age thinking – the erroneous notion that a different time period is better than the one one's living in – it's a flaw in the romantic imagination of those people who find it difficult to cope with the present."
~ Midnight in Paris

In the movie, *Midnight in Paris*, screenwriter, Gil Pender, and his fiancée are on vacation in Paris. He aspires to become a novelist and hopes to find inspiration to finish his first novel. She prefers him to stick with screenwriting where he is successful.

As he wanders the streets of Paris at night in search of inspiration, he is magically transported at the stroke of midnight back in time to the 1920s.

There he meets his favorite writers and artists from that era, such as Ernest Hemingway, Scott and Zelda Fitzgerald, Cole Porter, and Picasso, among others.

To accomplish this feat, Gil is driven by an intense desire to become a novelist and employs his creative imagination to this task with a clarity of purpose. The vivid image implanted in his mind creates a scenario that miraculously transports him across space and time to help him achieve his goal.

The role of the hero

The hero is the central character in a movie since it's his story being told. He's the one we choose to root for. For one glorious moment, he comes alive and casts a spell on us – we become him.

Even though movie characters may appear normal and real, they could not have existed without first being conceived in the mind of a creator. They have no reality or personality independent of a screenwriter, who breathes vitality and life into their being.

In fact, they represent the very life force of the screenwriter, who ultimately finds significance, meaning, and creative self-expression through them.

To be sure, a screenwriter may feel inspired to write a screenplay based on a germ of an idea planted in his/her mind.

Out of that seed will sprout a particular theme, story world, and cast of characters that bring to life whatever is needed for this concept to blossom.

Based on the central conflict in the story, the perfect hero soon emerges to find a resolution for it. Thus, the hero cannot exist without a particular conflict to resolve. One cannot exist without the other. The story is an outgrowth of the hero and vice versa. Each defines the other.

For example, the hero, Jake Sully, is better suited to his role in the movie *Avatar* than he would be in *An Officer and a Gentleman*. At the same time, Vivian Ward is more suited to her role in the movie, *Pretty Woman,* than she would be in *Erin Brokovich*.

Even though they are both heroes in their own right, their roles are specific to the genre and demands of the story being told.

Likewise, we are born to play a starring role in our own lives. Only we can play ourselves; it may require us to change personas or wear different masks at given times, but it's an art we must master if we wish to live well.

What does it take to be a hero? A hero is one who dares to participate in the eternal drama of life. He's the one who ventures forth alone and willingly sacrifices his life for others.

She's the one who can be counted on to act nobly and courageously in the face of incredible odds. She's the one who affirms life by willingly facing it.

He's the one who leads the way for others to follow. He's the one who sheds light on the darkness and makes the world less terrifying.

Metaphorically speaking, the hero is the one who scales the wall between the conscious and unconscious mind and steals fire from the gods.

"The artist's job is not to succumb to despair but to find an antidote for the emptiness of existence." ~ Midnight in Paris

The importance of storytelling

Storytelling has always been important to us. One can say it's part of our DNA. We thrive on stories; it's the way we have always communicated with each other.

It dates back to a time when our earliest ancestors sat around a fire and shared stories about their scary and thrilling experiences during the hunt. Sitting before a captive audience, they recounted their adventures while hunting the strange and savage beasts in the wild.

Because of their courage, instinct, and resourceful thinking, they were able to survive the hunt and return home with enough game to feed the tribe.

These stories were meant as cautionary tales of survival to emphasize the personal traits and qualities deemed most useful and valuable to the tribe.

They also provided models of behavior and ethics that members of the tribe could adopt and further develop to pass down to future generations.

Historically, our storytelling has been about humanity's struggle to tame the wild beast and wilderness outside and within ourselves.

Choosing to participate in this cosmic drama has embarked us on an inner and outer journey into the unknown. It's our active engagement in this so-called life that has allowed us to evolve and advance rapidly as a species.

Ultimately, it's our search for truth, significance, and meaning that has given us the impetus to keep evolving and striving to become the best version of ourselves.

Just imagine what unbelievable foresight and resolve were required for human beings to move from subsisting as disparate bands of hunter-gatherers to organizing themselves into a community of complex nation-states.

Throughout history, myths, fairytales, and folklore have served as a way to decipher life's mysteries and establish essential guiding principles for everyone to live by.

These stories are meant to ground us in the reality of our world and imbue our lives with meaning. They evoke a sense of awe and wonder surrounding the mystery of our existence.

How else could we cope with the cycles of birth and death – the seeming temporality of life? These stories help to insert meaning and purpose into our mundane lives.

Through our shared experiences, we have learned to empathize with each other and provide much-needed comfort during times of adversity. We have even created rituals to celebrate various important events in our lives.

Undoubtedly, our evolution has been driven by a deep-seated desire to fulfill our potential. This has led us to continually take stock of ourselves and question our belief system.

It's no wonder we find ourselves asking: What's the best life to lead? What will make us happy? What should we value? No matter how we answered these questions, we instinctively knew it was possible to fulfill our wildest dreams.

Birth of the hero

Even though the hero springs forth from the writer's imagination, she is born with a backstory. Like us, the hero is part of a greater matrix that includes a family and community.

Her temperament and ability to solve problems will most likely depend upon her upbringing, socio-economic status, natural abilities, and belief system.

This is the frame of reference informing her decisions and actions she takes over the course of the movie.

Initially, the hero may be experiencing a certain lack in her life requiring her to take action. She may possess a character flaw or weakness keeping her from experiencing the life of her dreams.

Since the hero was created to resolve a particular conflict, she can rest assured that concealed within the problem is the solution that will lead to her ultimate reward.

It's only by losing herself in the drama and playing her role authentically that she achieves her goal and discovers surprising truths about herself and life. She's the hero of her own story – the center of the world.

Whether by chance, choice, or necessity, the hero finds himself wrestling with the same existential questions we so often ask ourselves: Where did we come from? Why are we here? Where are we going?

More often than not, the hero forgets his purpose for being once he enters the arena of battle. He becomes overwhelmed by the conflict at hand and suffers an existential crisis.

Like us, the hero experiences loss, despair, grief, shame, guilt, fear, failure, loneliness, and death. He comes face to face with the limitations of earthly life and realizes how precious life is, yet, how transient.

When the hero sets out on an outer journey to pursue a goal, he must necessarily embark on an inner journey.

The outer journey takes place in the physical world, visible to both the hero and the audience. It's how we will gauge whether the hero succeeds or fails in achieving his goal.

The outer world is where he will be challenged and forced to fight his battles, while the inner world is where he will confront and, hopefully, overcome his demons.

The farther he travels in the outer world, the deeper he travels within the inner world – it's how he comes to know himself.

At some point, the moment arrives when the hero must confront his fears and slay the dragon barring him entry to the cave where the treasure is hidden.

By boldly facing the series of tests along the way, he develops the physical and mental capacity to confront any final opposition.

By overcoming his fears and slaying the dragon, he gains entry into his own soul. He experiences a moment of self-revelation and seizes the destiny designated for him at the moment of conception.

Thus, to transcend her circumstances, the hero must recognize that whatever she seeks is also seeking her.

It's this secret knowledge that enables her to unleash the dormant forces within her being and boldly confront any fate that might befall her.

By doing so, she becomes a fearless warrior and rewrites the script of her life. Life begins and ends with her. She claims the scepter of power.

> *"I believe that love that is true and real,*
> *creates a respite from death."*
> *~ Midnight in Paris*

The truth about stories

Stories reveal hidden truths about the vast unrealized potential of the psyche. In short, the unconscious mind translates knowledge about its true nature into a symbolic language, which is communicated to a storyteller's imagination who can bridge the gap between the conscious and unconscious mind.

The characters, settings, actions, and themes found in stories become the symbols and metaphors that relay the essence of these transmissions. The wisdom contained in stories serves as a guide through the passages of life.

Great stories offer potent insights about life that act as breadcrumbs leading us down the path of enlightenment towards ultimate fulfillment.

A great benefit of the reel world is that it opens a window onto the larger world for the audience to peer through. It shows us how others are coping with a range of complex issues in their lives.

It reminds us that we are not alone. It exposes us to other cultures and lifestyles, thereby expanding our horizon.

It challenges or may even strengthen our value system. It allows us to dream about myriad possibilities for our own lives.

Most importantly, it gives us a glimpse into the minds of our fellow human beings to see how they are making sense of the world. It broadens our frame of reference and imbues our lives with significance and meaning.

To be sure, the object of the hero's desire is merely a means to an end. What he is really seeking is not so much the thing itself, but what that desire truly represents: happiness, security, respect, freedom, justice, love, validation, or fulfillment.

When Gil goes on vacation in the movie, *Midnight in Paris*, he hopes to finish writing his debut novel and solidify his relationship with his fiancée. Instead, he finds unexpected inspiration to improve his novel and discovers that his fiancée was not the right partner for him.

Thus, the hero must be willing to transcend her circumstances by daring to turn her vision of the good life into reality. She must set a goal and take the necessary steps to achieve it despite myriad challenges.

Protagonist vs antagonist

One reason we are so captivated by the movies is watching how the hero changes over a specific period of time. The same evolutionary impulse that resides within humans and pushes us to become better versions of ourselves similarly impels the hero to act.

This impulse is triggered when an antagonist is introduced who is a gatekeeper or actively competes for the same goal as the hero. This opponent is there to test the hero and/or prevent him from achieving his goal.

Such opposition acts like a force of nature to push the hero beyond his limit. Finally, it strips away any mask the hero is wearing and forces him to confront his true identity.

Initially, it may be a burning desire for a particular goal or an inciting incident that forces the hero out of his comfort zone.

He may wish to gain the love of a woman or win a particular competition. He may wish to prevent a bad event from taking place or need to escape from some shady characters in hot pursuit.

He may embark on a quest in search of treasure or enlightenment. He may seek an elixir to heal a wounded land or a broken heart.

Whatever his objective, the hero must fully commit to his goal if he intends to succeed in his quest. By participating authentically in the drama, he reaps the greatest reward.

The hero not only gains the object of her desire but discovers something even more precious – the secret knowledge that true power resides at the center of her being – and can be wielded at will once she remains fearless in the face of adversity.

"What we do in life, echoes in eternity."
~ Marcus Aurelius

CHAPTER 2

LAW OF ATTRACTION

(A is for "Aladdin")

The Law of Attraction is a fundamental law governing the universe. It's no different from the Law of Gravity that states, 'anything that goes up must surely come down.' Yet, many people do not grasp this concept or simply refuse to embrace it.

One of the basic tenets of the Law of Attraction is "thoughts become things" or "like attracts like." It suggests that any dominant image held in mind with enough emotion, over an extended period, will materialize in the physical world.

It also means that if your outlook on life and thought patterns are continuously negative and self-destructive, you will attract people, events, and circumstances to make them come true.

The wisdom of the ages is that the reality out there is not objective and can be affected by your thoughts. In other words, your thoughts, feelings, and attitude generate their own vibrational frequencies and constantly attract things that match their energy.

In her bestselling book, *The Secret*, Rhonda Byrne states, *"Everything that's coming into your life, you are attracting into your life. And it's attracted to you by virtue of the images you're holding in your mind. It's what you're thinking. Whatever is going on in your mind, you are attracting to you."*

The truth is whether you believe in the Law of Attraction or not; it is constantly at work in your life, and chances are you are where you are today because of what you focused your thoughts on and channeled your energy towards. Like attracts like.

Thoughts are things

All thoughts eventually become things. Your thoughts are the objects of manifestation and require a powerful force to form them into physical reality. That force is the Law of Attraction.

It's not uncommon to find people struggling to grasp the concept of the Law of Attraction and how to manifest what they want in their lives. However, once you understand its principles, you can use them to achieve your dreams and fulfill your potential.

To understand the physics behind the Law of Attraction, you should be aware it rests on the bedrock of the Law of Vibration. Based on this law, it dictates that everything in the universe is in perpetual motion even though it's not visible to the naked eye. The frequency at which different elements vibrate differs between them.

Whether positive or negative, every thought you think has a specific frequency. The positive thoughts represent higher frequencies, while the negative thoughts represent lower frequencies.

Let's suppose you are thinking about buying a new house and are feeling very excited about it; this will cause you to vibrate at higher frequencies because you are extremely happy about manifesting your desire.

In turn, the Law of Attraction will match the frequency of your thoughts with the frequency of your desire and manifest it into reality through people, events, and circumstances. This is how the Law of Attraction turns thoughts into things.

"Be specific with your words.
The deal is in the detail." ~ Aladdin

The manifestation process

It is your conscious mind that initiates and controls the manifestation process. It impresses the subconscious mind with your heart's desire and vibrates to match the frequency.

In contrast, your subconscious mind is timeless and cannot tell if you are experiencing an event in the present moment or in the past. It's not logical. It responds to emotions. You manifest what you believe.

An early proponent of the Law of Attraction, Neville Goddard, states: "*All things evolve out of consciousness. The subconscious does not originate ideas but accepts as true those which the conscious mind feels to be true and in a way known only to itself, objectifies the accepted ideas.*"

There are three principles governing the Law of Attraction. The first principle of the Law of Attraction is "like attracts like." This means that things vibrating on similar frequencies are naturally drawn to each other.

The second principle of the Law of Attraction is "nature abhors the existence of a vacuum and will attempt to fill the void." In practical terms, it means that you cannot simply avoid negative thoughts and feelings; you must actively fill the void with positive energy.

The third principle of the Law of Attraction states that "life happens in the present moment, not in the past or future." Remember, negativity attracts negativity. If you are unhappy with your current life, you will attract more unhappiness. If you imagine a brighter future but continue to resent your present life, happiness will remain elusive.

You can improve the present by generating positive energy. It requires you to focus on the positive, practice gratitude, and act as if you already have what you desire. By taking these steps, you will improve your current situation.

A common misconception about the Law of Attraction is that it requires no action on your part. To materialize what you want, you only need to think hard enough and raise your vibrations. Nothing could be further from the truth.

The act of manifesting and the Law of Attraction are inextricably linked with action. In fact, it requires you to interact with the Universe. You're not a passive onlooker but a participant. Otherwise, it becomes little more than magical thinking and untethers you from a sense of reality.

"Genie magic is really just a façade. At some point, real character's always gonna shine through." ~ Aladdin

In the movie, *Aladdin (2019)*, the hero is a street urchin who finds an ancient lamp in a cave. He rubs the lamp and unwittingly summons a powerful Genie locked inside for centuries. He tells Aladdin that he has the power to grant him three wishes. The one caveat is his wishes must be specific.

Aladdin invokes the Law of Attraction by clearly stating his desires to the Genie. First, he wants to escape the cave where he is trapped, and second, he wishes to become a prince. He saves his third wish for a later date.

Aladdin is very clear-eyed about what he believes will make him happy. He displays a childlike faith in the Universe that his three wishes will be granted. However, he fails to consider the unintended consequences that will result from the fulfillment of his desires.

An important principle of the Law of Attraction is that to manifest a desire, one must feel the emotions of having that desire, right now. You have to imagine what achieving your goal will look like and feel like as if it were real.

What does finding your true love feel like? What does winning that competition feel like? What does driving that new sports car feel like? You have to rise in consciousness to become one with the object of your desire, right now.

If you still find yourself struggling to make the Law of Attraction work for you, below are five steps to raise your vibration and attract more positive energy:

Determine what you want

As simple as this sounds, it's shocking to discover that most people who complain about the Law of Attraction not working for them cannot even define what they want.

The first step to utilizing the Law of Attraction is to have a clear end goal that you want to achieve in mind. Your goal must be specific. Do you wish to start a new career? Do you wish to buy a new house? Do you wish to own a new car? Do you wish to find your soulmate? Whatever you desire must feel achievable in your own mind.

The Law of Attraction is not magic and does not work with wishful thinking. You need a destination to get to within a specific period and then work within the rules of the Law of Attraction to achieve it.

The best method to manifest your desire is to write down why you want it after you have chosen your desire. Take some time to write down your thoughts in a notebook or journal and explain why you want to manifest that desire.

For example, if you desire to find a new job, you can write that I want to manifest a new job so I can earn enough to cover my living expenses and live comfortably. I also want that job so I can take care of my family or buy a new car.

By doing so, you will be able to generate positive emotions when you think about why you want to manifest your desire. You begin to feel elated as you focus on having and enjoying your desire, which will raise your energy level.

Focus on positivity and gratitude

There's something known as self-talk that we often do on autopilot. We have a little voice in our head that constantly chatters to us, so imposing some positivity on it will go a long way in helping you manifest your dreams.

This voice can be either positive or negative. How many times have you used this voice to condemn yourself? You've probably lost count. It happens multiple times a day.

Allowing these negative thoughts and energy to build up in your mind can be counterproductive and hinder you from leveraging the full power of the Law of Attraction in many areas of your life.

Focusing on gratitude and positive self-talk will significantly increase your confidence and set you on the right path for success.

Make a list of the things you are grateful for. Let it serve as impetus to propel you from where you are to where you ought to be. Remember, you are not your thoughts – you are the Thinker.

"If you don't have anything, you have to act like you own everything." ~ Aladdin

Let your communication reflect your goal

When it comes to manifesting a specific outcome, you have to be fully focused on that outcome. Your everyday communication should exhibit your belief in what you are trying to achieve.

In other words, you need to start speaking and acting as if you've already attained your goal.

For instance, there's a massive difference between "I am" and "I will be." The former demonstrates you've already achieved your desire without an iota of doubt, while the latter sounds unconvincing.

Whether you agree or not, we are the product of our thoughts and words, so pick your words wisely.

The legendary boxer, Muhammad Ali, was known worldwide for his famous boast, "I am the greatest!" We all know what happened in the end. He went on to become the greatest boxer the world has ever known.

Notice how Muhammad Ali didn't say, "I will be the greatest." He knew of a principle that others were not aware of, and it is the same principle you are now learning right now. You can speak your own greatness into existence, too.

Besides visualizing your desire, you can write about its fulfillment in your notebook or journal. You can explain in detail the emotions you are feeling after finding a new job, or elaborate on the events and experiences you are having with your colleagues at your new job.

As you visualize your desire, believe you have already manifested it. You can do this by becoming a vibrational match with your desire. You must feel it in your core in order to generate the emotions to align yourself with your desire.

Visualize your success

One of the most critical aspects of the Law of Attraction is visualization. Successful visualization simply means simulating an image in your mind of how you will achieve your end goal right from the start.

It's like a mental movie of the process of how you will actualize the goal you are trying to manifest. In other words, visualization is seeing yourself already attaining that result.

It can be as straightforward as closing your eyes and seeing yourself following all the small steps you need to get to your destination. When you focus and follow this step to the letter, you are closer than ever to success.

Visualization should not take more than a few minutes a day – the amount of time needed to go through a mental movie or paint a mental picture of your achieving your desired result.

Trust the Universe

Once you have decided to follow all the steps above, trust that the Universe will work for you and propel you to manifest your desire. You must keep your thoughts and feelings positive at all times because when you feel good, you are surely on the path of your desire.

You need to be conscious and very focused here to ensure you don't take your eyes off the ball. Once you trust the Universe, it will open pathways for you through people, events, and circumstances to manifest your desire.

The concept of manifestation is closely aligned with the Law of Attraction. Since one principle of the Law of Attraction is "like energies attract like energies," then manifestation is about effectively channeling this power.

Therefore, manifestation is primarily about directing your intentions toward bringing your object of desire into existence. By thinking positively and engaging the principles and power of the Law of Attraction, you can manifest the life of your dreams.

"The point of power is always
in the present moment."
~ Louise L. Hay

CHAPTER 3

CONFLICTS AND CHALLENGES

(N is for "No Country for Old Men")

The Law of Attraction is an immutable force that attracts people, events, and experiences into your life. This universal law applies to everything in the Universe. It's been likened to gravity, but it's more accurate to think of it as a magnetic force that attracts like energy.

You can build the life you want using the Law of Attraction. The truth is that you are already manifesting your life with your current thoughts and emotions. The important thing to understand about the Law of Attraction is that it works regardless of whether or not you believe in it.

It will bring whatever you focus on into your life, but the problem is that most people don't realize how their thoughts create their own reality. This law is based on the principle of "like attracts like."

The Law of Attraction is working right now. You consciously and unconsciously attract everything you think and feel into your life. You are shaping the conditions of your life with the thoughts and feelings that you emit.

There are a lot of misconceptions about the Law of Attraction. Many people believe that it's a new age phenomenon solely for new agers and spiritual seekers.

It might surprise you to learn that the secret principles behind the Law of Attraction were known throughout the centuries by a small number of people but never revealed to the general populace.

Today, this knowledge is readily available and some people experience astounding success by correctly applying the Law of Attraction. To do so, they use their thoughts and emotions as a magnet to attract what they want in life.

But still, some people are unable to get their desired results even after applying the Law of Attraction for many years. They complain that it doesn't work for them.

Actually, the problem is not with the Law of Attraction; the problem is with the individual's incorrect application of this law.

If the rule you followed brought you to this, of what use was the rule?
~ No Country for Old Men

In the movie, *No Country for Old Men*, Llewelyn Moss, stumbles upon a briefcase full of money in the aftermath of a drug deal gone bad, while hunting in the desert. Anton Chigurh is a hitman hired to recover the money stolen by Moss. Ed Tom Bell is the local sheriff tasked with investigating the crime.

Moss thought that his dream of living the good life had finally come true, but little did he know it was about to turn into a nightmare. Undeterred, he takes the money and runs while Chigurh follows in hot pursuit

No matter where Moss hides, Chigurh relentlessly tracks him down because there's a tracking device hidden in the briefcase. Believing this is his lucky break, Moss has no qualms in risking his life to keep the money.

Meanwhile, Chigurh lives by his own rules. Once hired for a job, he stalks his prey to the bitter end. He has no respect for the law. He believes in fate and kills those he encounters on a coin toss. Chigurh follows Moss like his own shadow. Moss could not have chosen a more formidable foe.

Once the protagonist declares an intent to pursue a particular goal, he can rest assured that it will arouse some type of opposition in the form of an antagonist. This opposing force will arise to challenge and even block him from achieving his goal until he proves himself worthy.

Often, the hero reaches a point when it looks like all is lost. He hits a brick wall. He runs into a detour. A gatekeeper blocks the way. A dragon must be slain before he can enter the cave. The map he owns is useless. A trusted friend betrays him. His opponent is more cunning than anticipated. He is no match for the competition. Even his survival instinct deserts him.

Since life can be unpredictable, it's always a good idea to plan and prepare beforehand for any undertaking. If the hero is hunting for treasure, then she should obtain a map and supplies ahead of her journey.

If she is competing in a tournament, then she should prepare herself to display her prowess. If she is seeking true love, then she should trust her own heart. Her mindset should be on winning and overcoming any obstacles that are sure to be placed in her path.

Unfortunately, Moss was ill-prepared for the quest that he embarked upon. Even though he was willing to risk his life for an ephemeral dream, he proved no match for the competition. Hence, his antagonist was able to prevail over him.

Oftentimes, we are unaware of our true potential until challenged by the opposition. There's always someone or something waiting to push us beyond our limit. It's what brings out the best or worst in us. This seems to be life's way of testing our commitment to our goal.

On the other hand, we may find ourselves unwittingly assuming the role of Chigurh and self-sabotage ourselves. Then it becomes a real contest within ourselves as we struggle to overcome our fears and flaws that often surface and prevent us from achieving our goals.

When you set out on a journey to pursue your dream, you may unconsciously assign a certain value on what you hope to possess or achieve. Some people are willing to sacrifice their lives for their dream, which is the ultimate value that can be assigned. This is the point of no return – win or lose.

Regardless of the obstacle or challenge being confronted, it's usually there to act as a catalyst to push you to evolve and grow. It seems to be a necessary part of the journey.

By choosing a goal you intend to pursue, you stand at the center of creation. Your task is to command and reconcile the conflicting forces that reside within your world.

If you stand firm and remain centered within your being, you cannot help but achieve success. By doing so, you become a full participant in the creation process. This is how you discover your true power and fulfill your destiny.

All the time you spend trying to get back what's been took from you, more is going out the back door. ~ No Country for Old Men

Even so, there are many people who are unable to manifest their desires using the Law of Attraction for a variety of reasons:

Lack of intense desire

When you do not have the intense desire for your wish, it means that you are not really serious enough to manifest that wish. It's not the first priority in your life. It's merely an option for you. You may forget about it for days. You are not enthusiastic about doing the techniques.

People who do not have a strong desire will not apply the techniques consistently. After reading certain manifestation books, they will be enthused and encouraged to practice the techniques, but they will quit after a few days when their energy is exhausted.

Just because you don't see results from doing the Law of Attraction techniques doesn't mean they aren't working. The problem could be that you don't have an intense desire or that you're not doing the techniques consistently.

Trying to change your life by making a list of wishes and then trying to attract them with the help of the Law of Attraction does not work if you are not really serious and passionate about what you wish for.

And some people's wishes will alter regularly. If you change your wishes frequently, none of your intentions will be impressed on your subconscious mind.

When you decide to manifest anything, consider whether it is a genuine desire that comes from the depths of your heart. Trying to manifest something you don't want is a waste of time. You need to determine what you truly desire and then create the sensation of it being granted.

Things do not often work out for people who lack an intense desire or are constantly distracted by other things. The key is to hold the desire strongly in your mind and then not pay any attention to whether you're getting closer to it or not – just keep focusing on it.

When you are feeling passionate about something, you will do the techniques continuously, even if you are tired or have difficulty doing them. You will feel the difference in your life by doing those techniques than before when you were not doing them. This is how you know that the Law of Attraction is working for you.

First, you must have a very strong desire for something and be sure of what your goals are. The stronger your wish and the more intense your desire or want, the more quickly you can manifest it.

You have to feel it in every cell of your body that you really want it. Then you have to work toward your goal with all the power of mind and feeling.

Your thoughts are creative. When you focus on what you are seeking in life, you draw more of those things toward you. It's that simple.

Negative emotions

The most common reason many people cannot manifest their desire through the Law of Attraction is because of past painful experiences. These people feel as if it is impossible for them to manifest anything good into their lives because of these bad experiences.

If you have been trying to manifest something for a while now, and you still have not seen anything come to fruition yet, it is most likely that there is some sort of resistance blocking you. This resistance comes from past negative experiences.

When we hold onto past painful experiences, we continue to send out vibrations of pain and suffering, which match up with those same vibrations that were sent out when the original experience happened.

By holding onto these negative emotions, we are essentially keeping ourselves trapped in the same patterns of pain which originally caused these negative emotions in the first place.

When you are resistant to positive changes, you tend to push away what you want in life. You might be doing this without even knowing it.

What makes this worse is that when you resist something, you become a vibrational match to what you don't want in life. Thus, with every day that passes, it becomes harder and harder for that thing to come into your life.

Anytime you try to manifest your desires, you are going up against your resistance.

Your resistance becomes a magnet pulling you in the opposite direction of what you desire. It's not possible to receive what you seek if there is even an ounce of resistance.

The key to overcoming your resistance is by healing the painful experiences that created it. When we heal our painful experiences, they no longer have power over us. By doing this, we can finally begin to attract all the good things we desire into our lives.

The important step in healing your resistance is by releasing the pain from your past negative experiences. This is done by forgiving those who hurt you and then forgiving yourself for allowing it to happen.

Fear is also a reason why people are not able to manifest their wishes. They may be worried that if they don't trust in themselves or the power of the Universe, they won't get what they desire.

Another reason why some people are unable to manifest their wishes is that they feel a sense of lack, so they keep focusing on what they do not have in their lives instead of being grateful for all they already have.

Always speak positively about what you want in life. You cannot attract what you want in life if your focus is on the lack of it. What you focus on is what you will get. So, focus on what you want rather than what you don't have.

It will be easier for you to attain your wish faster when you do this. You should always remember that life is a mirror and reflects back at us whatever we think about. When we think negatively, life gives us more negative things, and similarly, when we think positively, life gives us more positive things.

Lack of persistence

You also need persistence and consistency if you really want to bring your dreams into manifestation by using the Law of Attraction effectively. You can't give up if something doesn't come easily or instantly. You have to stick with it until the end when everything is fine, just as you imagined it would be.

When things don't go the way you planned, it's easy to become discouraged. Persistent people don't give up easily; they are resilient when things go wrong and figure out how to move forward from their failures. They know how to bounce back from their problems, and they're not afraid of taking risks.

Even if you don't see any indicators of your desire coming true when using manifestation techniques, it doesn't imply the Law of Attraction isn't functioning. It is at work behind the scenes.

Well, age will flatten a man.
~ No Country for Old Men

Lack of belief

You don't need any special abilities or powers to manifest your desire – just a sincere belief in your ability to create what you want in life.

What is belief? It is the feeling you have when you close your eyes and see yourself in your mind's eye as if you have already achieved what you desire. It is not how you feel now, but it is a feeling of confidence and certainty you will have once you achieve what you desire.

Some people devote a few minutes each day to practicing manifestation techniques, and they spend the rest of their time thinking about the awful things that have happened in the past and producing negative thoughts on autopilot.

It means their new concept hasn't been imprinted on their subconscious mind and hasn't developed into a belief. Negative beliefs from the past are still kept in their subconscious, and as a result, negative thoughts are generated on autopilot without their awareness.

These accumulated negative beliefs must be replaced with fresh, positive beliefs relating to your desire. To do this, you must use manifestation techniques such as visualizing with positive emotion.

You may produce the feeling of your desire being granted when you can perform the visualization methods vividly and use all of your senses. This will place your subconscious mind into a receptive state to receive manifestations from the Universe.

Do not focus on how difficult it is for you to manifest your desire because this will only produce doubt within yourself and block you from receiving what you want.

When you feel doubt creeping into your consciousness, use visualization techniques to banish them out of mind. Likewise, you need to stay away from any negative thoughts and make sure you are always optimistic when doing visualization exercises.

You must visualize a clear picture of what you want. Engaging all your senses, try to "feel" yourself already having what you desire. This will produce feelings of joy and happiness which are compelling emotions that can attract what you want into your life.

For example, if you are trying to manifest a new relationship, you might want to start by visualizing how it would feel if that person were already in your life. What would she look like? How would he act? What emotions do you feel?

Because emotion is the language of your subconscious mind, you may impress your desire with your subconscious mind and make it a belief when you develop a strong feeling in your visualization.

When applying manifesting techniques, don't be concerned about how your manifestation will occur or through which route it will reach you. Concentrate solely on the end result. The Universal Mind will take care of the details.

When you have conflicting energies around a desire, it's usually because the desire is stated as a thing rather than around the feeling you will experience at the time of fulfillment.

Visualization methods allow you to develop a belief that your desire is on the horizon, which helps you feel more positive and be more open to receiving it. It will also help you overcome any fear or doubt surrounding your desire, which will ultimately make it easier for you to get your desire.

You can also use positive affirmation techniques along with visualization for manifestation. Saying affirmations out loud is much more powerful than saying them silently in your mind. Affirmations are an excellent way to change your thoughts and beliefs.

Some people do not obtain the desired results because they do not employ affirmations appropriately. When using affirmation techniques for manifestation, the affirmation phrases should be written in the present tense.

For example, if you want to manifest abundance in your life, you would use the affirmation phrase: I am abundantly wealthy and happy.

When you write an affirmation phrase in the future tense, "I will be wealthy and happy," you are not expressing a sense of wealth and happiness now, but rather at some point in the future (which may never come).

It is also essential that your affirmation phrases are written to express positive emotions. The Law of Attraction responds best to positive emotions, so anything you wish to attract into your life, such as wealth, health, love, and happiness, should be expressed with feelings.

Be a force of love as often as you can, and turn away negative thoughts whenever you feel them surface.
~ Wayne Dyer

CHAPTER 4

ART OF PRAYER

(I is for "It's a Wonderful Life")

P rayer is the ultimate bridge between you and the Divine. When you worship God, the Universe, or Divine Spirit, you signify your trust and belief in a higher power.

Worshipping a Higher Power is an essential practice in most cultures around the world. The power of prayer is especially crucial in challenging circumstances since it pushes us to seek divine guidance.

Prayer is any type of saying that will connect and allow you to hand over your fears and challenges to a Higher Power. It creates a connection between you and God. You kneel in awe before the One whom you believe loves you unconditionally and makes all things possible.

The magic of prayer lies in the belief of receiving compassion, unconditional love, and endless support from the Universe. It empowers you to grow into a self-assured, powerful, and compassionate human being.

What is prayer?

Prayer is a summons that fosters an intense intimacy with God. It provides a powerful sense of emotional and psychological security. When you pray you strengthen your bond with a supernatural force capable of bringing about desired changes in your life.

Prayer is a source of insight and inspiration through which we become optimized and motivated to move on with our daily engagements. It fortifies our faith that we are not alone because there is an ultimate force to guide and protect us throughout our lives.

When you pray, you know that a way can be created out of impossibilities. Prayers let us win over tough battles and get over our negative thoughts, which are a big hurdle on our way to success.

Prayers enhance our hope and faith in those divine powers that protect us from all the dangers.

Remember, prayers are not just words you communicate to the Divine – your positive thoughts reflect you in action.

Why do we pray?

Prayers require complete faith in the power and abilities of the Universe. It is a form of spiritual practice and an act of obedience that allows you to connect with your higher Self and discover inner peace.

Through the power of prayer, you find solutions to your problems and learn to forgive those who have wounded or committed a grave sin against you.

Prayers are performed to express deep gratitude to the Creator who has blessed you with endless opportunities. Daily prayers can help you to become a wiser and more compassionate human being. It provides you with the mental strength and resilience to overcome any life challenges that confront you.

Through prayer, you seek God's forgiveness for all your sins and wrongdoings. You ask for His blessings and protection for your loved ones. It also significantly reduces your anxiety and stress levels.

Power of prayer

Prayer is a way to win over tough battles and get over your negative thoughts, unkind actions, and sinful feelings towards yourself and others.

It reveals your soul and brings light to the darkness that lies within you – the darkness of your pride, ego, jealousy, selfishness, and anguish.

Prayer can help you better understand those supernatural powers that protect you from all threats. You can feel the presence of a Higher Power in your body, mind, and spirit.

Even though we don't always verbalize our prayers during a crisis, our naked fear, despair, and hopelessness act as silent prayers of petition that summon the Universe to act.

"Dear Father in Heaven, I'm not a praying man, but if you're up there and you can hear me, show me the way."

~ It's a Wonderful Life

In the movie, *It's a Wonderful Life*, George Bailey lives in the small town of Bedford Falls. He manages the Bailey Building and Loan Association, a company founded by his father. George discovers that his absent-minded uncle has misplaced some funds at a time when the bank will be audited.

George suffers an existential crisis. He has dedicated his life to helping his community but stands on the precipice of ruin through no fault of his own. He considers himself an honest man, but the bank audit will expose him to be a fraud. He can't bear to face the imminent humiliation and disgrace.

He decides that the only way out of his dilemma is to take his own life. At least his wife will collect on his life insurance policy.

He gets drunk at a bar and recklessly crashes his car. Intending to take his own life, he stumbles towards a bridge over a raging river.

Before he can take the plunge, however, another man falls into the river. Without thinking, George jumps in and saves him from drowning. He learns that the man is his guardian angel, Clarence, who was sent on earth to save him as a way to earn his wings.

When George announces that he wishes he were never born, Clarence takes him around the town of Bedford to show him the reality of life without him. He is horrified to see that his town is a bleak place to live. The wife he cherishes remains an unmarried woman, which means none of their kids was born.

George learns a valuable lesson – to live is an individual act of heroism. The world he knows cannot exist without him. No one else can play his role better than him. He's not only the hero of his own life but a supporting player in many people's lives.

Similarly, we must be willing to follow our own path like real life heroes. Out of all the variables in life, here we are for one glimmering moment in time. We remain necessary beings at the center of existence. Once we hold true to your vision, the Universe invariably bows to our command.

After all, we are the ones giving it life and form, singing its praises, worshipping its creations, acknowledging its beauty, feeling its emotions, and expressing its potentiality. It's the way we find significance and meaning, and vice versa.

Life is forever striving to become the things, events, and experiences that we seek to witness in our lives. Without our conscious awareness and participation, life's potential will remain void and unfulfilled.

"I want to live again!"
~ It's a Wonderful Life

Benefits of prayer

What are the benefits of prayer? Why is prayer such a big deal in religious communities? Why all the fuss to get people to pray? Prayer is how people on earth give the supernatural permission to intervene in human affairs.

This permission is one of the underlying reasons why prayer is imperative for believers. Indeed, until we pray, we assume a posture that tells the Universe we can handle our affairs independently.

Prayerlessness says to God, "I can handle this on my own; I am strong enough." The truth is we are not. We are not strong enough to do life on our own without a Higher Power's strength, wisdom, and guidance.

So, what are some specific benefits of prayer?

Peace

In the Bible, Psalm 55:22 says, "Cast your burden upon the Lord, and He will sustain you..."

Prayer is an effective way of achieving peace. Peace is not the absence of conflict but the presence of calmness and safety amid chaos.

When the worries of life burden us, we have the option of taking our cares before the Lord and having him resolve them for us rather than by ourselves.

When we are faced with life's challenges, prayer offers us an avenue to ensure that we are not overwhelmed. God's ears are attentive to every prayer offered up by His children.

It makes no sense why we will choose to go about our lives carrying our burdens and worries and cares and pains and fears and disappointments when the Creator has offered to handle them for us.

Grace

Prayer does not only give you peace when it is offered; it provides you with the strength to wade through the murky waters of life's troubles. Another benefit is that prayer allows for the inspiration of God to solve the issues we face.

Whether it is healing for ourselves or a loved one, or we need the wisdom to think through issues we face, we can come before the Lord in confidence that He will come to our aid.

When we approach the Divine in prayer through faith, we do so because we are confident that God can come through with His supernatural hand and extend grace to help us along the way.

Wisdom

"But if any of you lacks wisdom, let him ask of God, who gives to all generously and without reproach, and it will be given to him." James 1:5.

If prayer is talking to God at its basic level, we see how wisdom is a direct benefit of prayer. The people we communicate with regularly tend to rub off on us, eventually. Now, imagine having a conference with the infinitely wise one regularly.

Indeed, your perspective on life will begin to change incrementally, and before long, you realize you are being described as wise.

Biblically, wisdom is seen as the alignment of our worldviews with that of God. We only get to achieve this lofty and impressive height through prayer.

"Strange, isn't it? Each man's life touches so many other lives. And when he isn't around he leaves an awful hole, doesn't he?"
~ It's a Wonderful Life

How to pray effectively

How does one go about praying effectively? While everyone should pray, everyone must know that there are right ways to pray and some ineffective ways to pray. Prayer length is not a determinant of effectiveness.

We cannot run before we can crawl. Take small steps until you have built up enough courage, confidence, and relations with God to spend more time with him.

Persist in prayer

"Devote yourselves to prayer…" Colossians 4:2. This simple line from Paul's letter to the Colossian church tells us that prayer is to be a lifestyle for the believer.

A consistent prayer life is necessary if you seek to have an effective prayer life. Most people give up on prayer after a few days or weeks of unanswered prayer. But that is wrong; we are to continue in prayer. That's how our spiritual muscles are built to ensure that we can receive the answers to our prayers.

Change your view on prayer

For most people, prayer is a means of laying requests before God. While this is not a wrong view, it is a short-sighted view if we only see prayer like that. Prayer is not supposed to be a shopping experience at the supermarket of heaven, with every person bringing their list of needs.

Prayer is supposed to stem from an earnest desire to be with God, savor his presence, and delight in Him.

When we come to see prayer this way, we will not only enjoy prayer when we receive answers but will yearn to pray because the Divine Spirit that we encounter in prayer is infinitely more valuable to us than the requests we make of Him.

Get in your word

"And now I entrust you to God and to the word of His grace, which can build you up and give you the inheritance among all those who are sanctified." Acts 20:32.

The Word of God is an essential foundation for effective prayer. This connection to the word makes the alignment of your will with the Divine will critical. If you knew the things God knows, you would only do the things God does.

Getting in on the will of the Divine is an excellent way to know what to pray for at what time. It also helps you to understand what things are accessible to you and how you can lay claims on these promises.

"Therefore I tell you, whatever you ask in prayer, believe that you have received it, and it will be yours." ~ Mark 11:24

Morning prayer

Starting your day with prayer is the best thing to do. Prayer gives you the strength and willpower to do things right. It has the power to guide you effortlessly through the day. It keeps you tranquil and promotes emotional wellbeing.

Prayer is a wellspring of insight and inspiration. You become better optimized and motivated to tackle your daily activities. Belief in a Higher Power gets strengthened and you start receiving blessings in whatever you do.

It fortifies your faith that you are not alone since there's an omnipotent spiritual force that guides and protects you throughout the day.

"God speaks in the silence of the heart.
Listening is the beginning of prayer."
~ Mother Teresa

CHAPTER 5

POWER OF IMAGINATION

(F is for "Finding Forrester")

The power of imagination is the ability to create something new in the world. It is perhaps the most significant key to achieving success. The fact is you can do and create whatever you wish if you only use your imagination.

We are given this power right from the moment we are born and this power never ends. We can take any object around us and use our imagination to reshape it into whatever we want it to be – a boat to go sailing, a stool to sit on, an airplane to fly away.

When we employ our imagination in this way, we are constructing reality from our thoughts. Everything that exists in the physical world has first been imagined by someone else's mind as an idea before coming into being as an object or as matter existing in space-time.

It's not only things around us but also the people around us that have been created from our thoughts using our imagination.

You can use your thoughts as an imaginary friend to help you achieve success in business and relationships. Positive thoughts attract positive experiences and events into your life, while negative thoughts attract negative experiences and events into your life.

Creating a new reality

You can even create realities beyond your own physical limitations with the help of imagination.

We all have the ability to create our own reality. The world we live in is a product of our imagination. What we imagine, we can achieve. This amazing concept has been discussed by great philosophers throughout history.

In fact, the power of imagination is so strong that it's literally changing our physical reality by creating it from nothing. And once you understand how this works, you can simply imagine things into existence with a realistic expectation of their appearance in your life.

The creative force within each of us is so powerful that it literally creates whatever we focus upon with our thoughts and emotions.

It is easy to observe that most people are using their imagination against themselves. They imagine things that will attract failure, gloom and doom into their lives.

As a collective consciousness, we have imagined all of these things into existence on a global scale over recent times. When enough people truly believe something, it begins to manifest in reality by drawing more people into this shared vision.

Live the life of your dreams

The power of your imagination is not as unrealistic as you might think; in fact, it's the first step to living the life you want.

The power of imagination can create any reality you choose to have. Imagination is a skill that few people use to its full potential. If you imagine yourself achieving a goal, then a series of events will take place that leads you to that goal. There are many examples of this power in action.

Imagination is the power of perception and creation. It is a mental state of consciousness involving an independent interpretation of reality. It's characterized by the synthesis of new ideas, thoughts, concepts, values, or solutions to problems.

The imagination enables us to envision things as they might be in the future and as they have never been known or seen before.

Imagination is a very powerful force that can create a better life for you and help others as well.

"Someone I once knew wrote that we walk away from our dreams afraid that we may fail or worse yet, afraid we may succeed."
~ Finding Forrester

In the movie, *Finding Forrester*, a black teenager, Jamal Wallace, befriends famous writer, William Forrester, after winning a dare. They both happen to live in the inner city; however, Forrester is a recluse and never leaves his apartment. The meeting proves fortuitous for both of them in more ways than one.

After winning a full academic scholarship to attend a prestigious private high school, Jamal is beset with doubt about whether to accept it. Forrester takes him under his wings and mentors him. This helps Jamal improve his writing skills and develop his own identity as he navigates high school.

Jamal could have easily become trapped in the inner city where he grew up and become a statistic. Instead, he uses his imagination to transcend his circumstances and envision a better life for himself. It was only a matter of time before the right people, events, and circumstances would appear for him to manifest his dream.

Meanwhile, he discovers that Forrester is a Pulitzer prize-winning author of a famous novel who never published another book. Jamal challenges him to use his imagination and overcome his fears. By remembering a happy event in his life, Forrester finds the courage to move back to his homeland.

Our belief system acts as a filter for our thoughts. What life requires is that we breakout of the mental prison limiting our power. Once we have a desire, unless we believe it's possible, we will never achieve it. Rather, we wind up manifesting the opposite because we focus more on the things we fear and don't wish to enter our lives.

You must become single-minded in creating beauty and order out of the chaos surrounding you. Treat your mind as if it were a blank canvas, and like an artist, use your palette to paint only the images you wish brought to life.

This is how you become a deliberate creator of your reality. By trusting the laws of the universe, you break free of all limitations. It is the anchor that will ground your being as you step into the vast unknown.

Why we struggle

When we struggle to turn our thoughts and ideas into something tangible, it's because there's a conflict with our imagination. It's not that we have forgotten how to be creative; it's that a diminished imagination has affected the quality of our thoughts. It's no wonder we feel stuck.

There are two key factors that stifle and limit our creativity. The first is when our ability to suspend disbelief is lost. We constrict our vital faculties and discount all that's no longer real or possible. Essentially, the only thoughts and ideas we allow to surface are the rational ones.

Allowing our life to grow stagnant is the second factor. We already know that our life experiences drive creativity, so when our imagination feels stuck, it means we need to try something new. We need to actively seek out novel life experiences.

How to cultivate your imagination

An effective exercise to reinforce imagination begins by strengthening your capacity to visualize. We frequently take our potential to imagine something in our minds for granted, whether it's an image, smell, or sound.

Although we are born with this ability, it takes a lot of work and repetition for most of us to get it right.

What comes to mind when you close your eyes and attempt to imagine a delectable dessert at your favorite restaurant? Do you only see a black screen with light squiggles zipping around? Or do you see enough details of your dessert to make your mouth water?

Don't worry if you didn't have a Pavlovian reaction to the dessert you imagined. This simple exercise can help you improve your visualization skills.

Begin by looking at an object in your home or business. It may be a piece of fruit, your computer, or anything else you can observe for 30 seconds. Close your eyes after 30 seconds and try to picture that object in as much detail as possible.

After 30 seconds, close your eyes and try to picture that object in as much detail as you can. If you have trouble recalling an image with your eyes closed, practice for 30-seconds every day for a few days until you become better.

When you've mastered the 30-second visualization technique of an object, imagine an entire scene depicting a favorite place you've visited or one of your best memories.

Repeat this step until it becomes second nature. Finally, imagine something that does not exist or a location that you have never visited. Practice this method at least once a day.

"Seasons change young man, and while I may have waited until the winter of my life, to see the things I've seen this past year, there is no

doubt I would have waited too long, had it not been for you." ~ Finding Forrester

Create a life you love

In a world where we have been programmed to believe that the physical world is all there is, it's hard to imagine that what we can't see can impact our lives. We might even think of imagination as the ultimate dreamer's pursuit, but the truth is that our mind's eye is a powerful tool for creating a life we love.

How does this work? By using our imagination, we are able to tap into a part of ourselves that "knows" or feels what we want. Our imagination helps us get in touch with this knowingness and then finds ways to manifest it in the physical world.

This doesn't mean that we have to imagine something and it will come true without any effort on our part. It means that when we use our imagination, we are permitting ourselves to make what we want a reality.

In doing so, we open up more opportunities for our desires to show up in ways that align with who we really are.

Thoughts are things

When you're able to tap into your imagination, you're also tapping into your intuition, which means that your deepest desires will be easy for you to recognize.

The ability to imagine isn't only a myth. If you think about something long enough, it will materialize. The world around you is made of energy. That energy follows your thoughts and turns them into something tangible.

You can think about anything for as long as you want, and it will happen because everything around you is made out of energy, and your thoughts create that energy.

Locking yourself into success through imagination has been proven time and time again by successful people. The more vivid and detailed your mental images, the better the results will be.

"No thinking – that comes later. You must write your first draft with your heart. You rewrite with your head. The first key to writing is...to write, not to think."
~ Finding Forrester

Neville's power of imagination

According to notable philosopher and author, Neville, God is pure imagination – God is your consciousness. The truth is that your imagination has the power to change your reality. He says, *"Nothing comes from without; all things come from the subconscious."*

You don't have to be wealthy to be happy; nonetheless, great wealth requires great imagination. Alternatively, you can live a life with minimal material possessions while still being able to explore the world using your wonderful imagination.

You will understand that all things subject to you are your fate. Your current state is a created imaginal act. With the power of the Universe, you can shape your morning, noon, and night as you wish.

Neville encouraged everyone to construct their world from the inside out rather than from the outside in. Describe yourself as you would like to be perceived by others, then act as if your words are true.

If you want to improve your life, you must become conscious of the ideas you are planting in other people's minds. Introduce a positive concept to someone who is in a negative state of mind when you meet them.

Thereafter, you must think she is uttering uplifting and positive words. This way, you can travel the world without being bothered by the negative thoughts of others.

Furthermore, if you wish to manifest a desire, you must begin a motor activity to make it appear as if it has already manifested. In this way, you can draw your desired state closer to reality. This process brings your imagination to life.

You have the ability to get from where you are to where you want to be based on your desires. Because your imagination shapes your reality, if you want to improve your life, you must become conscious of the ideas you plant in the minds of others and yourself.

Your ability to manifest isn't limited to the present moment. Because time does not exist in the metaphysical realm, you can use the power of imagination to change your life.

This is the story of your life, your experiences, and thus your reality. You have complete control over your life since you are the creator. This is a groundbreaking notion by Neville that you can use to live a more congruent existence.

The transformation process begins with the desire to change, after which you train yourself to concentrate and control your thoughts in the way you desire.

Once you are able to cultivate your imagination, you can successfully use the power of your awareness to create your own reality.

"The great secret is a controlled imagination, and a well-sustained attention firmly and repeatedly focused on the object to be accomplished." ~Neville

CHAPTER 6

THE SCRIPTING METHOD

(E is for "Eat Pray Love")

How do you manifest the life of your dreams when you believe the world is against you? You've heard the saying, "life is what you make it," but you're still not sure how to turn your life and fortune around. What if I told you everything could change with a few simple steps?

Let me introduce you to the revolutionary practice of scripting. Scripting is an essential key to manifesting your dreams. You have been given the power of manifestation from birth, but you may not be using it.

Scripting gives you the power to create a reality that reflects who you are and what you want in life. It's an amazing tool to create your ideal life. It's a way to rethink your reality.

What exactly is scripting?

The scripting method (sometimes known as future journaling) is a popular Law of Attraction technique that helps you visualize a reality in which your dreams have already come true.

The process involves writing down your ideal life and allowing yourself to assume an author or screenwriter role, dramatically detailing this desired reality in a story-like fashion through words.

As the recent bestseller, *The Secret*, states: "Everything that we think or do is creating our future." Scripting is a great technique to engage with manifestation because it allows you to let your imagination go wild and write about what you want your life to be like as if it already exists.

Does it really work?

Journal writing is a powerful tool for helping you materialize your thoughts. Writing down what you wish to manifest helps clarify your intentions and reframe your existing reality.

In essence, scripting is a form of visualization but takes the process one step further. This is what renowned author, Jack Canfield, has to say about the power of visualization in his book "The Success Principles":

"When you visualize your goal as already complete each and every day, it creates a conflict in your subconscious mind between what you are visualizing and what you currently have. Your subconscious mind works to resolve that conflict by turning your current reality into the new, more exciting vision."

So, if the technique of envisioning your ideal future has such a powerful impact on your subconscious mind, just imagine the level of transformation that can take place when you add scripting into the mix.

The act of writing things down is extremely powerful. Author, writing coach, and speaker, Allison Fallon, recounts in her book "*The Power of Writing it Down*" how her life was transformed when she discovered the power of daily writing practice.

She believes that writing is one of the most powerful tools we have for unlocking our lives and notes in her book that scientific data reveals that writing for just five to twenty minutes a day can help you in the following areas:

o Identify your ruts and create new neurological grooves toward better habits.

o Find fresh motivation and take ownership of your life.

o Heal from past pain and trauma.

o Relieve anxiety and depression.

o Contextualize life's setbacks and minor frustrations.

o Live a more confident, balanced, and healthy life.

o ...and so much more.

Hopefully, you are persuaded that combining these two practices will make a significant difference in your life. So, let's see how you can apply this practice to your daily life and start making the changes you wish to become a reality.

"We search for happiness everywhere, but we are like Tolstoy's beggar who spent his life sitting on a pot of gold, under him the whole time." ~ Eat Pray Love

In the movie, *Eat Pray Love*, recently divorced Liz Gilbert decides to take stock of her life and embark on a journey of self-discovery. By charting her own course, she discovers the pleasure of food in Italy, the power of meditation in India, and true love in Bali. By facing her immediate fears and misgivings, she carves out a new life that turns out to be much more fulfilling than the one she leaves behind.

Liz finds herself at a crossroads after her marriage ends. Rather than fall to pieces, she sets a new plot in motion by invoking the law of cause and effect. Her quest is to return balance to her world. The way to achieve her objective is the problem that she must resolve.

Liz moves fearlessly from place to place in search of the missing pieces of her life. Although things appear somewhat chaotic on the surface, Liz can rest assured there is a carefully drawn plot underpinning her every move.

It's the reason she cannot give up too easily because inherent in every problem is the correct solution. Only her response to the outcome is under her control. By remaining open to new possibilities, Liz discovers her true Self.

The best time to script

You are probably aware of the huge benefits of a morning routine, and indeed, you may already have one in place that might include things like reading or meditating.

Although it can be done at any time of the day, it's not essential to script in the morning. However, I would recommend making scripting a part of your morning routine if you can.

When it comes to the question of how often you should script, there are no hard and fast rules. It should become a habit for you. You should practice scripting every day so that you get used to making the time and feel more of a flow right from the start.

On the other hand, if you have specific goals and dreams that you wish to achieve, I would suggest that the bigger they are, the more often you need to be scripting.

You don't have to make it complicated, and you can script whatever aspect of your life you feel most passionate about writing.

You may want to write about different areas of life or different parts of the same goal. Each day can be as specific or as general as you wish it to be.

One word of advice, when you're starting out, decide on a set time that you will commit to and write it down in your journal.

Once it becomes a habit, you won't even need to think about it, but when you are new to this, it helps to have a set time written down in your journal as an appointment with yourself that you need to keep.

How do I start?

It all begins with a vision. If you don't already have one, try this...

Sit down with a journal and a pen. Take some time to think about the next twelve months and the changes you want to see for this to be the best year of your life and ask yourself these questions:

- What do I want in my family?
- What do I want in my job?
- What do I want in my relationships?
- What do I want in my health?
- What do I want in my finances?

There are all sorts of goals and aspects of your life you might think about, but these are just a few.

Not everyone has a solid vision of what they want from life. If that's you, then simply start scripting how you want to feel first and go on the journey from there to begin to script what you want your life to look like a year from now.

In truth, you may not have big goals right now, but this technique can work for you even if you just need to feel better and more confident or happy in life.

Start to imagine how grateful you feel about your unique life and the wonderful friendships you have or about how fit and healthy you feel, or how much energy you have. Then write it down.

Once you start to make a daily habit of scripting in this way, you will be amazed at how your feelings start to change and align with the version of yourself that you are visualizing and writing about every day.

"You are after all, what you think. Your emotions are the slaves to your thoughts, and you are the slave to your emotions."
~ Eat Pray Love

Transforming your future

Choose to either write a more general script or take a specific aspect of your life and start to let your imagination run wild with thoughts and feelings about your desired reality in that area.

Don't write in a detached way, but immerse yourself in the feelings and emotions of what you are writing. Allow yourself to feel the fullness of what reaching that goal or having that thing would feel like to you.

The Law of Attraction is not just about attracting what you think about, but about how you feel, which is a critical aspect of implementing this technique.

It might sound like a lot of work and a big commitment, but writing down these scripts each day should not take long. Once you commit to practicing it regularly, it will become an enjoyable habit that can change your life.

"You need to learn how to select your thoughts just the same way you select your

clothes every day. This is a power you can cultivate. If you want to control things in your life so bad, work on the mind. That's the only thing you should be trying to control."
~ Eat Pray Love

A few more useful techniques

In addition to scripting, there are also significant benefits from journaling about your day. Writing down your thoughts and feelings helps you gain clarity on what is going well in your life, as well as what might need a little tweaking.

This process can be very cathartic if done correctly and can help manifest your goals. You can write down things that are going well and what isn't working so well in your life right now.

You can also create Wish Lists – writing out your wishes for various aspects of your life to enable you to give focused attention to those things and aid in manifesting them.

This will kickstart your imagination into overdrive. It also enables you to see how you can improve your experiences solely through your thoughts.

It may also help to create an evening journaling ritual before bedtime. Review the events of the day and jot down any concerns, anxieties, or fears you may have.

The simple act of getting those things out of your head and down onto paper is a great way to put an end to the swirling mass of thoughts.

Often, once they're transferred onto paper, the things we worry about seem much smaller and more manageable than when they're whirling around in our heads.

Practicing this ritual before bedtime guarantees that you will be calm enough to get a good night's sleep.

Believe your dreams are within reach and that it's time for you to start scripting and journaling your way towards the life you desire.

"Efforts and courage are not enough without purpose and direction."
~ John F. Kennedy

CHAPTER 7

ART OF MINDFULNESS

(S is for "The Secret Garden")

Mindfulness is a state of being that allows us to be fully conscious of the present moment. There are no thoughts in our minds in this state. The only thing that remains is awareness. This state is considered a "mindless" state.

During meditation, we are silently and alertly watching our thoughts in the present moment without passing judgment. This is what mindfulness meditation is all about. Mindfulness refers to any activity that is carried out with a high level of awareness and alertness.

What is mindfulness?

When we are born into this world, we have no mind or memory. Nothing is stored in the memory of a child. She moves from one moment to the next without being distracted by her thoughts.

Every moment is filled with excitement for a child. If a child finds even a stone, she will be delighted and play with it. To her, everything is a surprise.

There is no memory, no knowledge, and no thought in this condition. There is nothing left but pure consciousness. This is the wonderful state of being happy.

This was the biblical state of Adam in the Garden of Eden until he was tempted to taste the fruit of the Tree of Knowledge.

The true master is awareness. The mind is the servant. When a child matures, his mind expands, and his knowledge expands. The difficulty begins right here.

He gradually loses awareness. He becomes enslaved by his own thoughts. The servant is elevated to the position of master. Without our control, the mind continues to generate thoughts.

The mind is a tool and must only be used when absolutely necessary. However, once we lose control of our mind, it begins to work on its own. All activities are carried out mechanically as if we were robots.

While we are engaged in an activity, our minds think about something else in the background that we are utterly unaware of. Mindfulness is the process of regaining our mastery, recapturing our lost consciousness, and reclaiming our childhood.

The difference is that the child lacks the ability to think. We move beyond the mind when we practice mindfulness. The mind is still present and we can employ it with awareness anytime we choose.

To become mindful, we must strive to conduct all of our activities with awareness and attention. We will often lose track of our awareness and perform the activity mechanically while thinking about something else. But as time passes, we become aware of the situation.

Meditation can assist us in achieving this state of mindfulness. In meditation, we must sit comfortably and observe our thoughts without passing judgment.

"If you look the right way, you can see that the whole world is a garden."
~ The Secret Garden

In the movie, *The Secret Garden*, a young orphan, Mary Lennox, is sent from India to live with her reclusive uncle in a castle in England. Being left in the care of his servants, she spends her days rambling around the gloomy castle and discovers a secret garden.

The garden once belonged to her deceased aunt but was locked away after her death. Mary decides to restore the garden to its former glory as a secret project, with the help of a boy, Dickon, who lives on the estate.

One night she follows the sound of someone crying and discovers a new cousin, Colin, who is bedridden and kept hidden in his room. She secretly visits his room every day and brings him into the garden for fresh air. The more Colin spends outdoors, the healthier he becomes.

Mary's faith in his ability to walk inspires Colin to believe in himself. Eventually, he becomes strong enough to surprise his father by running into his arms when he returns home after a trip. Thus, Mary restores life in the garden and love in the castle.

Mary reminds us that we all need a "secret garden" where we can escape and regenerate ourselves. It should be a place of beauty and tranquility where we can find solace and solitude. Such a sanctuary must be created deep within our being where we can withdraw from the stimuli of the world.

Our thoughts are like waves on the surface of the ocean, while stillness and silence are to be found beneath its depths. The way to access this dimension is by foregoing all mental activity. Stillness is the gateway to our center of power, where past and future do not exist, only an eternal now.

As human beings, we possess an uncanny ability to imagine the outcome of whatever we desire and then simulate the emotions we expect to experience once it materializes. This is what gives us the confidence to dream the impossible dream.

We can recreate our reality by changing the pattern of our habitual thoughts. The past does not exist in reality, except the memories and impressions left behind. The future is still to come and depends on the thoughts we choose to think, here and now. This instant is our point of attraction.

Importance of mindfulness

Our entire lives will become a meditation if we do everything with awareness. We can easily count how many times we have missed our awareness today and how we have suffered as a result.

As we practice mindfulness, our state of unawareness gradually fades and we achieve complete mindfulness.

Our mind will be a servant to us once we have achieved complete mindfulness. It will complete all tasks we assign it with greater efficiency than before. As we become more in tune with the universe, we will automatically be pushed towards the dreams we desire.

Our thoughts will have great power. We don't need to seek fame and fortune. It will come to us on its own. Our talks will be fruitful. We will not waste time chatting or engaging in activities that are not productive.

The benefits of mindfulness-based actions will grow and become more precise. We acquire the ability to pass judgment on those around us. We sense what is going on in the mind of the person speaking before us.

The world will appear more beautiful and magical. People and circumstances that are positive will be attracted to us. Positive traits will develop within us and the negative features will be eliminated.

Peace, love, and happiness will continue to increase. All fear, hatred, and jealousy will disappear.

"You brought us back to life, Mary. You did something I thought no one could do."
~ The Secret Garden

Mindfulness techniques

Mindfulness can be practiced in a variety of ways. We begin with our bodies in the first technique. Make an effort to become more aware of your body. Keep an eye on your bodily movements, which are mechanical in nature as if you were a robot.

Make those movements more conscious. Everything you do, such as moving your hands, rubbing your eyes, walking, sitting, and speaking, should be done with mindfulness. Attempt to move your body in a mindful and alert manner.

After becoming conscious of your body, the next step is to become aware of your thoughts and how they operate. The mind is a feature of the human brain. A thought pattern creates a neural pathway in the brain.

How does the mind generate ideas? What is the pattern of your thoughts? How often does a specific thought come up? How does one thought lead to another? Simply bring your thoughts into awareness. The mind will produce fewer thoughts as you bring more awareness to it.

The next phase is to monitor your feelings and moods by moving closer to your heart. The mind is more subtle than the body. Thoughts are more evident than emotions and moods.

As a result, it requires little effort at first. However, with effort, you can become more conscious of your moods and emotions.

When the first three stages have been completed, a fourth stage will occur on its own. Complete consciousness is the fourth step. It's known as self-awareness or spiritual enlightenment. Once we reach this level, we will no longer be the same person.

We must come to terms with the truth. We need to realize that we are not separate parts; we are whole. According to Buddha, the only thing you can carry with you after you die is your consciousness. That's the true wealth.

Who am I?

Ramana Maharshi from India is one of the great masters of this century. He devised the technique of Who Am I? It's a direct path to discovering your true Self.

This technique involves a thorough inquiry of one's true Self. However, it should not be a verbal one. If we ask a question verbally, we will only obtain a verbal response. The true answer, on the other hand, isn't a word. It's a realization. It's an understanding.

Therefore, our question must be a feeling. When we ask profoundly and with feeling, we will eventually discover that no one can answer our questions. Then we will realize that the question is the answer to the question itself. That is who we truly are.

Self-remembering

George Gurdjieff, a Russian mystic, introduced a technique known as self-remembering. He compares man to a machine. He performs all of the tasks in a sleepy state because he has forgotten himself.

When you see something, you become completely immersed in it. You've lost track of the subject. You are the subject.

His message is to always remember you. It shouldn't even be a thought. It has to be a feeling. You'll realize that your thoughts aren't you after that sensation has settled in.

There will be no thought or mind if you thoroughly anchor yourself in that self-remembering. Then comes the transform-ation. The awakening takes place.

We already have our true selves within us. However, due to our mind's delusion, we have yet to realize it. This mind is the stumbling block. We will realize our inner Self once we comprehend how to let go of the mind.

"That's the thing, isn't it. Loss changes people". ~ The Secret Garden

What is Intuition?

It is not uncommon for people to act intuitively once in a while without even knowing they just acted based on a "gut feeling." Intuition is often referred to as the "sixth sense," which allows us to correctly discern a situation and make appropriate decisions without the use of logical or conscious reasoning.

How to leverage the power of intuition

The five senses possess relatively limited abilities, with each having a specialized set of receptors that transmits specific impulses. We can feel things only when touched. We can hear sounds in the distance. The eyes have a far greater reach and can even see the moon and stars.

Our intuition or sixth sense works in a completely different way. It has no connection to the five senses since it's not part of them. While the functionality of other senses, such as hearing and visual acuity can be measured, we cannot measure intuition.

There's a reason that intuition is not as developed as other senses since it's not meant for decoding information from the outer world. Its main purpose is to enhance our lives and make us understand our true nature.

After all, there's no point in having "closed eye" intuitive capability only to see what our eyes are designed to see. Intuition is a subjective ability and is not subject to extensive scientific analysis.

An effective way to start paying attention to your subconscious and learning to trust your intuition is by becoming more aware of those subtle voices from within that seem to pop out from nowhere.

While our conscious mind makes use of logic and is relentless at it, our subconscious combs through the past, present, and future while striking connections with our feelings and hunches in a nonlinear way.

Follow these steps to train yourself how to live more intuitively:

Write down your thoughts

You can start keeping a journal to write down your thoughts and feelings. Stick to it even when it appears you don't have much to say. Doing this regularly will help clear any blockage and open up your subconscious mind.

Shun your inner critic

Remember you are trying to do something different from what you are already used to. So, forget about trying to rationalize the voices that pop up within you. Let inner dialogue flow without interruption or fear.

Retire to a quiet place

Finding the perfect setting that allows for the free flow of emotions is critical to discovering and nurturing your intuition. You should be able to strike an emotional connection with a specific color, music, or object – anything that triggers the flow of feelings from within.

Doing these three routines regularly will help you develop clarity of the mind, build a deeper connection with the "Self," and bring real, intuitive awareness to your daily life.

"Plenty of people miss their share of happiness, not because they never found it, but because they didn't stop to enjoy it."
~ William Feather

CHAPTER 8

MANIFEST YOUR DESTINY

(T is for "Trading Places")

You were born into this physical world to forge your own path and destined to face unique life events and circumstances. You were born with divine powers and the ability to shape your own life into anything you want it to be.

Your higher Self already knows what you want and where you need guidance, and all you have to do is unlock your inner potential to manifest your desires. You have the power to change your destiny through your divine consciousness.

Your reaction to your current circumstances helps to define you. No matter how challenging, every situation reveals a different aspect of your being. The choices you have made in the past have shaped your life up to this point.

The thoughts you allow to take root in the present moment will determine your future. Once you are in harmony with your being, the world appears in full accord with your destiny.

Once you have decided to manifest your destiny and work according to its guidance, you will find yourself being successful in all areas of your life experiences and be able to work with purpose.

Thoughts and the Law of Attraction

You might have heard before that thought is power. This means that thought is a form of energy, and when you think a thought, it radiates out to the universe.

There is a very close relationship between your thoughts and the Law of Attraction because your thoughts are the objects of manifestation, and they require a powerful force to take form into your physical reality, and that force is the Law of Attraction.

How thoughts become things

Whether it's a positive thought or a negative thought, every thought has a specific frequency. The positive thoughts represent higher frequencies, whereas the negative thoughts represent lower frequencies.

Let's say you experience an intense desire to buy a new house and feel quite certain that one day you will buy it and live in it. In that instant, you will vibrate through higher frequencies because you feel ecstatic and confident about manifesting your desire.

In turn, the Law of Attraction will match the frequency of your thoughts with the frequency of your desire and manifest it into your reality through people, events, and circumstances. This is how the Law of Attraction turns thoughts into things.

"Just be yourself, sir. Whatever happens, they can't take that away from you."
~ Trading Places

In the movie, *Trading Places*, Billy Ray Valentine is a homeless man hustling in the streets to survive, while Louis Winthorpe III is a successful commodities broker, living the good life. One day, their paths cross when they are randomly selected by Louis' wealthy and powerful uncles, the Duke brothers, as part of a social experiment.

The Duke brothers argue the merits of nature vs. nurture, unsure which one really makes the man. As part of their experiment, they make a wager with each other to find out if Billy Ray and Louis traded places; whether either man will survive in his new environment.

To make things more authentic, they frame Louis as a thief and publicly expose him before other social club members. He is fired from his job, and his bank accounts are frozen. When he returns home, Louis finds himself locked out of his house, which is owned by the Dukes. Finally, he loses his fiancé and is ostracized by his friends.

Meanwhile, Billy Ray is a quick study on the job and employs his street smarts to stay competitive. It soon becomes obvious that Billy Ray is well-suited to his new position as a trader. It's a defining moment in his life and paves the way for him to fulfill his destiny.

On the other hand, Louis is having a hard time adjusting to his new life, which involves living on the margins of society. It becomes clear that Louis will not survive the experiment without outside assistance. He unwittingly becomes a case study of what happens when the affluent lose their wealth, power, and privilege.

Billy Ray and Louis act as perfect foils for each other when their roles are reversed. Who can tell whether this random act by the Dukes was not in alignment with Billy Ray's secret desire? One thing is certain, he was ready when opportunity knocked on his door. The same quick wit and resourcefulness he employed to survive in the streets proved most valuable on the job.

In the meantime, Louis does not fare too well since there is nothing in his background that prepares him for abject failure. Having to live at a subsistence level creates cognitive dissonance that clashes with his self-image. This is why for the greater part of the movie, he expends his energy on exposing Billy Ray as a fraud to regain his status in society.

Everyone is born into the world with certain assets and liabilities that determine their place in society. These assets may include a close-knit family, education, unique talent, wealth, good looks, athletic prowess, or charisma.

On the other hand, some people may grow up with certain disadvantages, such as a dysfunctional family, poverty, illiteracy, addiction, or physical disability. Of course, there's no guarantee that possessing a particular feature will ensure one's happiness, or having a certain liability will preclude one from enjoying a good life.

Everything depends on how well you use your assets and whether you can turn a liability into an advantage. After all, wealth, beauty, and genius contain their own form of suffering and never guarantee their recipients a happy life.

Therefore, when you set a goal, in reality, what you are doing is secretly hoping to 'trade places' with the new person you intend to become. By participating authentically in the drama, you will not only gain the object of your desire but will tap into the omnipotent power at the center of your being.

How to use the Law of Attraction to manifest your dreams

Everyone has a dream, but only a few people successfully manifest their dreams into reality. This is because most people are unaware of the fact that they have unlimited potential to make their dreams come true or hold limiting beliefs regarding their dreams.

If you have a dream, you can easily manifest it by using the Law of Attraction by thinking about your dream life and how you wish it to be. When you start imagining your dream life, you will enter into the zone where you begin to raise your vibration and align yourself with your dream.

"Think big, think positive, never show any sign of weakness. " ~ Trading Places

Here are some powerful ways to take control of your life and manifest your destiny:

Practicing meditation

Meditation is a highly effective practice that helps you go deeper within and understand your true Self. It is one of the best ways to manifest your destiny as it will help calm your mind and increase your vibrational level. You will be able to think more clearly and generate more ideas.

You may practice meditation to connect to your divine spirit or higher Self and start focusing on where you want to be. Begin imagining what your new destiny looks like and how it feels to accomplish it. You must clearly acknowledge it through your senses and emotions within.

Begin affirming to yourself, *"I am going to change my destiny and I know that I can manifest what I want to be. I am connected to divine spirit and it will be guiding me wherever I go. I am moving towards the path of my dream, and all universal forces are working in my favor."*

Once you affirm what you want, start taking action and work according to your goals, and you will be amazed by the astonishing results. It will feel like a supernatural force is pushing you towards a different path. Your thoughts and feelings will begin to change their pattern, and you will experience a range of emotions as you shift towards your new destiny.

Connecting with divine guidance

There is a great power that lies beyond your thinking and imagination and that is divine guidance. You are surrounded by these divine forces and must align yourself with them.

Ask them to provide you with wisdom and knowledge to achieve your goals and manifest your destiny. To quote the New King James Bible: *"Ask, and it will be given; seek, and you will find; knock, and it will be opened to you."*

Removing the limiting beliefs

To manifest your destiny, you must first remove the limiting beliefs you hold in your mind because they hamper you from taking significant steps in your life. They also create a negative pattern of thoughts in your mind.

You must replace those limiting beliefs with a positive mindset to lead you towards the successful completion of your goals.

Since thoughts become things, you must think positive thoughts and hold positive beliefs to create positive results that take you towards the path of your destiny.

Following your intuition

Always follow your intuition whenever you are going to manifest your destiny. Your intuition is the inner guidance that will give you the urge to take specific actions towards your destination.

Trust your intuition and follow it. It plays an essential role in one's life as it always takes you towards the easiest path to manifest your dreams.

Visualizing your perfect destiny

Begin your day by taking a moment to visualize your perfect destiny. Imagine how you want your life to be and where you want to be.

Visualization will help you better focus on your goals and destiny by creating a strong connection between you and your destiny.

By visualizing what you wish to manifest, you are sending out powerful signals to the Universe and it cannot help but respond to you. It will help you overcome barriers and open new pathways for you to fulfill your destiny.

"The advice I would give to someone
is to not take anyone's advice."
~ Trading Places

How to change your destiny

Many people think that the events and the experiences in their lives are predestined and cannot be changed. That's not true. You are a divine being who possesses a divine spirit within you. You need only align yourself with divine consciousness through which you can change your future experiences.

You may practice meditation to connect to your divine spirit or higher Self and begin focusing on where you want to be. Imagine what your future will look like. Clearly acknowledge it through your senses and feel the emotions within.

Start affirming to yourself that you have the ability to change your destiny and can manifest whatever you wish to be. You are connected to your divine spirit and it is helping you wherever you go. You are moving towards the path of your dreams, and universal forces are always working in your favor.

Final Words

Manifesting your destiny is a crucial step to take in your life as it provides you with an awareness of your true potential. It allows you to fully explore the contrast between living a normal life and living a life of true purpose. It provides new ideas and opportunities for you to live a meaningful and significant life.

You are the Creator of your own destiny and possess a divine potential that is available to you all the time. You can live your life with confidence, knowing that your inner spirit and divine consciousness are there guiding you every step of the way.

"It is not in the stars to hold our destiny but in ourselves."
~ William Shakespeare

REFERENCES

Byrne, Rhonda. *The Secret.* Hillsboro: Beyond Words Publishing, 2006.

Canfield, Jack. *Success Principles: How to Get from Where You are to Where You Want to Be.* HarperCollins, 2015.

Fallon, Allison. *The Power of Writing It Down: A Simple Habit to Unlock Your Brain and Reimagine Your Life.* Zondervan, 2021.

Gawain, Shakti. *Creative Visualization: Use the Power of Your Imagination to Create What You Want in Your Life.* Nataraj Publishing, 2002.

Goddard, Neville. *Power of Imagination: The Neville Goddard Treasury.* Penguin Group, 2015.

Tolle, Eckhart. *Stillness Speaks.* Novato: New World Library, 2003.

Internet Sources

Wikipedia. *Wikipedia (Online Encyclopedia).* <http://www.wikipedia.org/>

MOVIE LIST

M - Midnight in Paris

A - Aladdin (2019)

N - No Country for Old Men

I - It's a Wonderful Life

F - Finding Forrester

E - Eat Pray Love

S - The Secret Garden

T - Trading Places

.

ABOUT THE AUTHOR

Primrose Roberts is an author, spiritual coach, and digital marketer, who has a deep fascination with the realm of metaphysics, myths, and manifestation. Having discovered the Law of Attraction at an early age, she has spent her life studying its principles to learn how it can be used to guide our lives, manifest our dreams, and craft the lives we've always wanted.

The author has a passion for the art of storytelling and screenwriting, and uses her knowledge to inspire her readers to embrace the Law of Attraction and make their dreams a reality. As a dedicated Seeker, she strives to decipher the link between storytelling and manifestation to understand how you can become the hero of your own story.

For more information about the author and to receive future updates, please visit her website at: https://primroseroberts.com.

Other Book Titles:

The Metaverse: Reimagining Race in the Changing World Order

Course Offered:

Advanced Manifesting: Master the Law of Attraction

https:/advancedmanifestingacademy.com/

Dear Reader:

Thank you for purchasing my book. As an indie writer, your support makes a huge difference. If you enjoyed this book, please take a moment to leave me a review and share it with your friends and family. It will be greatly appreciated. Thank you.

Warmest regards,

Primrose Roberts

https://primroseroberts.com/
https://advancedmanifestingacademy.com/

ADVANCED MANIFESTING

Made in United States
North Haven, CT
05 July 2022

20971229R00074